If anyone ever asks me
what part of my life you are,
I will just look at them
and smile and say,
"The best part."

The happiness you give me
is something I'll never be able
to get enough of.

I love having you in my world.

And I love having you
to love.

I Love You
Soooo Much

A book for my soul mate...
and a thanks from my heart

by Douglas Pagels

SPS Studios™

Boulder, Colorado

Library of Congress Catalog Card Number: 2001005733
ISBN: 0-88396-616-6

Certain trademarks are used under license.

Manufactured in Thailand
Second Printing: September 2002

 This book is printed on recycled paper.

Library of Congress Cataloging-in-Publication Data

Pagels, Douglas.
  I love you soooo much : a book for my soul mate—and a thanks from my heart / Douglas Pagels.
      p. cm.
   ISBN 0-88396-616-6 (alk. paper)
  1. Love poetry, American. I. Title: I love you so much. II. Title.
   PS3566.A3372 I16 2002
   811'.54—dc21

                                                                    2001005733
                                                                          CIP

SPS Studios, Inc.
P.O. Box 4549, Boulder, Colorado 80306

I love you

You have so many things no one else will ever have.
You have all my love — now and forever.
You have my admiration — for being such
    an incredibly precious person.
You have my unending gratitude — for the way
    you brighten my life.
You have my hopes — all gently hoping you know
    how glad I am that you warmed my world
and touched my very soul.
You have my every affection.
You have my desires and dreams.
You even have things there are no words for.
You have whispered words that belong to you,
    thoughts you have inspired, and blessings that
    have touched the deepest part of my heart.
You have the most beautiful wishes the stars
    and I can wish, and my prayer that someday
    I'll be able to thank you for all this.

You have a standing invitation to share the days
with me ~ and to be the one and only
person who holds the key to my happiness.
You have arms I want around me, eyes
I want to lose myself in, and a joy in
your voice that I could listen to forever.
You have empty pages in the story of your
life ~ pages I'd like us to write together...
filling them with memories we'll make
and stories that will travel beside us
and carry us over whatever comes along.
You have my sweet appreciation ~ for taking
my smiles places that my heart has only
dreamed of.
And you'll always have me,
my "thank ~ God ~ for ~ you" feelings,
and soooo much love.

I am so glad that you are a part of my life. It is such a privilege ~ to know you, to share myself with you, and to walk together on the paths that take us in so many beautiful directions.

I had heard of "soul mates"
before, but I never knew
such a person could exist ~

until I met you.

Somehow, out of all the twists and turns our lives could have taken, and out of all the chances we might have missed, it almost seems like we were given a meant~to~be moment ~ to meet, to get to know each other, and to set the stage for a special togetherness...

When I am with you, I know that I am
in the presence of someone who makes my
life more complete than I ever
dreamed it could be.

I turn to you for trust, and you give it openly.
I look to you for inspiration, for answers, and for
encouragement, and — not only do you never let me
down — you lift my spirits up and take my thoughts
to places where my troubles seem so much further
away and my joys feel like they're going to stay in
my life forever.

I hope you'll stay forever, too. I feel like you're my
soul mate. And I want you to know that my world
is reassured by you, my tomorrows need to have you
near, so many of my smiles depend on you,
and my heart
is so thankful
that you're here.

I Am So in Love with You

No one ever touched my life like this.
No one in all the seasons of sweetness
and sadness and everything in between.
No one ever came so close to being the
coming true of this gentle and wonderful dream.

No one else knew the way to all the
warmth within my heart, and yet...
you just seem to naturally know
not only how to go there, but how much
I want you to stay.

I am in love with you because
you make me sing and dance
and smile and celebrate
and hope... and believe.

I love you because
no one ever did
what you do...
for me.

It would bring me more joy than I can say
if you would never forget
    ~ not even for a single day ~
how wonderful you are...
        in my eyes and in my heart.

I'm so often at a loss to find the words
to tell you how much you mean to me.
In my imagination, I compare you with
things like the sunshine in my mornings,
the most beautiful flowers in the fields,
and the happiness I feel on the best days
of all.

You're like the answer to a special prayer.
    And I think God knew
        that my world needed
            someone exactly like you.

If I know what love is, it's because...
I know you. You are the reason for
so many of the smiles I have, and
you're the one place my heart always
wants to go — when it wants to feel
hopeful and grateful and glad.

If I know what love is, it's because my
thoughts of you have such a
    beautiful way

       of gently filling my soul...

My thoughts of you are my mornings' inspiration and my evenings' comfort. They are wondrous thoughts, free in spirit, and they take me along when they're soaring above the things that cloud other parts of my life. You make everything all right in my world, every time I think of you.

If I know what love is, it is because every moment with you is a past, a present, and a future that brings me closer to a wish come true than any fantasy I've ever had. With your own special magic, and in your own marvelous ways, you have given my days more richness and joy and love...

than most people
   will ever dream of.

I love having you in my life. It has never been the same since you came into it, and I know it will never be the same again.

I love you so much. You are always inside me, warm within my heart, and you are everywhere in the world that surrounds me. You come to me tenderly.

You take my soul places it's never been before. You give me more of you than I ever knew anyone could give.

You give me feelings that feel like presents almost too beautiful to open. Among the gifts you have given, one of the most wonderful of all is the joy of being so close to you. Thank you for trusting me enough to share all that you are... with all that I hope to be. I love catching glimpses of every new facet you share. And the more you do that, the more I can't help
but adore what I see...

In the time that we have been together, you have made my sun rise on so many mornings — and I'm sure it was you who made my stars come out at night.

You've surprised me with the gifts of hope and laughter and love, and you've made me a believer in something I never used to have too much faith in: the notion that dreams really can come true.

If there are times when you look at me and see my eyes filled with smiles, it's only because my heart is so full of happiness and because

my life is so thankful for
...you.

The nicest feeling I've ever known
is being in love with you.

And I want to thank you
for these feelings...

For bringing me happiness
as though it were a gift
I could open every day
...I thank you.

For listening to all the words
I want to be able to say
...I appreciate you.

For letting me share the most
    personal parts of your world
    and for welcoming me with
      your eyes
            ...I am grateful to you.

For being the wonderful, kind,
    giving person you are
          ...I admire you.

For being the most beautiful
    light in my life
          ...I desire you.

For being everything you are to me
    and for doing it all so beautifully
          ...I love you.

The things I promise to be for you

A place you can come to for comfort.
Eyes you can look at and trust.
A hand to reach out and clasp.
A heart that understands
and doesn't judge.

A supportive shoulder to cry on.
A long walk anywhere you want to go.
And for any time when we're apart:
a close and caring intimacy
that you will always know.

A door that is always open. A caring,
gentle hug. A time that is devoted to
you alone.

A reflection of my love.

Every time I say I love you...

I'm really trying to say
so much more than just those three little words:
I'm trying to express so many
wonderful feelings about you.

I'm trying to say that you mean more to me
than anyone else in the world.

I'm trying to let you know that I adore you
and that I cherish the time we spend together.

I'm trying to explain that
I want you and that I need you
and that I get lost in wonderful thoughts
every time I think about you.

And each time I whisper "I love you,"
I'm trying to remind you
that you're the nicest thing
that has ever happened to me.

I've never felt this way about anyone before

I want you to know so many things about my feelings for you. It used to scare me a little bit to know how open I have been with you. Before you came along, so many of my inner feelings were completely mine. I didn't think I would ever find anyone I could trust enough to share them with. But now, so sweetly and assuredly, I have. I am so incredibly glad you're here.

And now... you know so much about me. Things that, for the first time in my life, I feel safe sharing. I guess I just knew that you had a caring heart that would take wonderful care of the things that are so important to me.

Now there is a connection between us that will always be one of the most meaningful things I'll ever be blessed with. The place where my life lives alongside yours is my sanctuary.

It is a space where an unbreakable bond exists between us. It's the one place on this planet where my path converges with the path of another, where I can be close enough to walk alongside you on your journey and have you there to walk with and talk with on the journey of all my days.

You know where I hide the keys to the doors that lead to my happiness and my hopes. You have been with me in moments of closeness so complete that words get lost and love gets found in everything. You know the highs and lows, the dreams, the memories, the way yesterday has been, and the way I want tomorrow to be.

There are many things that no one knows... but you. And today, I want you to know this, too: No matter what the rest of the world might have planned, I want our lives to continue on... with the sweetest understanding and the strongest connection any two people can share.

Do you know how important you are to me?

I know you probably wonder
from time to time
what you mean to me.
So I'd like to share this thought with you,
to tell you that you mean the world to me...

Think of something you couldn't live without
...and multiply it by a hundred.
Think of what happiness means to you
...and add it to the feelings you get
on the best days you've ever had.

Add up all your best feelings
and take away all the rest...
and what you're left with is
exactly how I feel about you.

You matter more to me than you can imagine
and much more than
I'll ever be able to explain.

Will Love Last?

One of the most valuable lessons we can learn from life is this:

That, try as we might, we will never have all the answers.
We can wonder for the rest of our days whether we are
doing the right thing... continuing in the best relationship
and following the best paths toward tomorrow, but no one
is ever going to answer those questions for us.

We both may have wonderings of what to do and curiosities
of what's to come. Time will help us with the results, but
more than any one thing, it's up to us — and to the love we
have for each other — to go in the right direction.

You and I might sometimes wonder about where we're headed
and whether our love will last a lifetime through. We may
not know the answer, but I'll tell you the one thing I do know:

There's no one
I'd rather try to spend
forever with... than you.

Love Endures

There are few miracles in this universe as amazing as love. When it is true and real and lasting, it forms an unbreakable bond between two very fortunate people. It lets one know that it is always there, always caring. It lives in the deepest part of the heart, but it sneaks out as often as it can... to inspire a grin on the face, a smile in the eyes, a serenity in the soul, and a quiet gratitude in the days...

Love is giving and forgiving, taking and partaking of the sweetest joys and most comforting reassurances imaginable.

Love can work wonders. It can travel a thousand miles in the span of one second, and it can take every hope and well-wishing along with it on the journey. Love can feel at home no matter where it is, as long as it knows that it has a companion there by its side to make each place, each day, and each moment a space and a time of sharing.

Love is amazing, precious, and beautiful. It's there for the giving, here for the receiving. Love is what I want to give to you and what I pray that you will always share with me.

Love endures, and love will make sure that we're as happy as two people can be.

A Little Love Story

I love you. So much. And so amazingly.
Each day is like a new page that I get
the privilege of turning over, with a new
paragraph for the morning, a sweet entry
for the afternoon, and a can't-wait-to-read
romance that winds its way to the brightest
stars anyone ever wished upon...

Ours is a story of two people, each with a journey in search of a distant horizon. Two souls whose paths were allowed to cross, whose words felt right at home, and whose smiles discovered that walking the way together could lead to a kind of happiness that only comes along once in a lifetime.

We were given a gift that many people search all their lives for and never manage to find. When I found you, I just knew how I wanted to fill the empty pages of my life.

I want to be with you... and I want this love story to have a very happy ending...
by never, ever ending at all.

If I didn't have you, I don't know what I would do. For with you, I have so much. Such sweetness. And happiness. And love.

You are a rare combination of so many special things. You bring me feelings that know no limits, and smiles that never go away. You are a part of every day of my life, whether you are close enough to touch or out of reach to all but my hopes and my dreams.

In everything, it seems like my life was just waiting for you. And with you here, I want you to know that I have never been so happy...

I love you for understanding me the way you do. And for caring. You have created lasting changes in my life and in the way I want tomorrow to be.

You have given me the courage to express what I feel inside. We have shared thoughts that have brought us together and that will keep us there from now until the end of time.

Our love is a gift that will forever be.

Thank you for being mine.
    And thank you... for loving me.

I don't know exactly what it is... but there is something very special about you.

It might be all the things I see on the surface, things that everyone notices and admires about you. Qualities and capabilities. Your wonderful smile, obviously connected to a warm and loving heart. It might be all the things that set you apart from everyone else.

Maybe it's the big things: the way you never hesitate to go a million miles out of your way to do what's right. The way your todays help set the stage for so many beautiful tomorrows. Or maybe it's the little things: words shared heart to heart. An unspoken understanding. Sharing seasons...

Making some very wonderful memories.
The joys of two people just being on the
same page in each other's history.

If I could ever figure out all the magic that
makes you so special, I'd probably find that
it's a combination of all these things —
blended together with the best this world
has to offer: friendship and love, dreams
come true, strong feelings, gentle talks,
listening, laughing, and simply knowing
someone whose light shines more brightly
than any star.

You really are amazing.

And I feel very lucky to have been given
        the gift of knowing
             how special
                 you are.

I care about you so much.

And that caring and that feeling
have a meaning that is more precious
and more special to me than
   words can begin to describe.

But let me try to tell you this...

Saying "I care" means that I will always
   do everything I can to understand.

It means that I will never hurt you.
It means that you can trust me...

It means that you can tell me
   what's wrong.
It means that I will try to fix what I can,
that I will listen
when you need me to hear, and that ~
even in your most difficult moment ~
   all you have to do is say the word,
     and your hand
       and my hand
    will not be apart.

It means that whenever you speak to me,
whether words are spoken through a smile
   or through a tear...
    I will listen with my heart.

Inside of me there is a place...
where my sweetest dreams reside;
where my highest hopes are kept alive;
where my deepest feelings are felt;
and where my favorite memories are
      tucked away, safe and warm.

My heart is a lasting source of happiness.
Only the most special things in my world
get to come inside and stay there forever.

And every time I get in touch with the
hopes, feelings, and memories in my heart,
      I realize how deeply
                  my life
            has been touched by you.

If there's such a thing
as "meant-to-be"

...then every day
I grow more
sure that we're
in that
miracle-on-earth,
dream-come-true,
"somebody-must-have-known
how-much-I-needed-you"
category.

What Is Love?

Love is a wonderful gift. It's a present so precious words can barely begin to describe it. Love is a feeling, the deepest and sweetest of all. It's incredibly strong and amazingly gentle at the very same time. It is a blessing that should be counted every day. It is nourishment for the soul. It is devotion, constantly letting each person know how supportive its certainty can be. Love is a heart filled with affection for the most important person in your life. Love is looking at the special someone who makes your world go around and absolutely loving what you see.

Love gives meaning to one's world and magic to a million hopes and dreams. It makes the morning shine more brightly and each season seem like it's the nicest one anyone ever had.

Love is an invaluable bond that enriches every good thing in life. It gives each hug a tenderness, each heart a happiness, each spirit a steady lift.

Love is an invisible connection that is exquisitely felt by those who know the joy,
    feel the warmth, share the sweetness,
        and celebrate the gift.

It would take me a lifetime to list
    all the reasons why
you are so important to me.

It would take me forever to find words
for all the thanks I would like to express...
for all the deeply reassuring feelings I have
    felt in your acceptance of me.

And it would take an eternity to
    give you back even half
    of the happiness you've given me
    during the wonderful times we've shared...

But until forever is here,
until a lifetime is lived,
and until eternity gives me a chance
    to say everything
        my smiles try to show...

I will hold you in my heart
    more gently than any feeling,
I will keep you on my mind
    more lovingly than any thought, and
I will feel blessed by your presence
    more than you will ever know.

I receive so much joy from just being
able to see a smile in your eyes.
I love to look at you and realize how
incredibly glad I am for what we have
and everything the
      two of us share.

I need those moments in my life.
I need your goodness and your giving
     and all the memories we've made.
I need the promises and the plans
and the precious gift of simply
     holding your hand in mine.

It would be wonderful if all the wishes
I could ever imagine could find a way
to come true. But deep down inside,
I don't need all those wishes.

    All I need... is what I have
      with you.

You are my own special miracle.

The days we share are my blessings.
The memories we make are my treasures.
The togetherness we have is my dream come true.
And the understanding we share is
    something I've never had
        with anyone but you.

If anyone ever asks me
what part of my life you are,
I will just look at them and smile and say,
"The best part."

The happiness you give me
is something I'll never be able to get enough of.
I love having you in my world.

            And I love having you
                to love.

I find that you're on my mind
more often than
        any other thought.
Sometimes I bring you there
        purposely... to console me
                or to warm me
                    or just to make my day
                        a little brighter.

So often you
surprise me, though,
and find your own way
        into my thoughts...

There are times when I awaken
and realize what a tender part
    of my dreams you have been.

And on into the day,
whenever a peaceful moment
seems to come my way
and my imagination is free to run,
it takes me running
        into your arms
            and allows me
                to linger there...
knowing there's nothing I'd rather do.

I know that my thoughts are only
reflecting the loving hopes of my heart...
because whenever they wander,
        they always take me
            to you.

♥ Miracles Really Do Come True

I think that we have been given some of the most beautiful presents this world has to give. We have the joy and strength and support of being true companions, and we have all the feelings and special meanings that treasure brings, all the "knowing why" and the "understanding when." We have a sharing instilled in us — and a kind of caring that words can't describe.

No matter how high the walls may be between other people, there is an open door between us that always leads to love, and a window that looks out upon a beautiful view...

    a miracle that
        keeps on coming true.

I Will Always Love You

I am going to love you all my life,
through whatever comes along. The
feelings I have will stay strong and
true, knowing that our tomorrows
hold so much promise for us.

I really think that you and I have an
opportunity to be as happy as any two
people could ever be. That's why this
is what I would wish for, if I could
have just one request...

Please...
   just keep on loving me.

Because no matter what comes along,
   if we just keep our love strong

we can always
work out all the rest.

You are the love of a lifetime
I've always wanted as mine,
and you are the special soul mate
I always hoped I'd find

You are my very own, one perfect person:
everything I always hoped for... my secret
dream that swept me off my feet and really
did come true.

You have the warmth of the morning sun in
your spirit, and you have a gentle soul that
I want to always be close to. I deeply, dearly,
and happily love you!

I can barely begin to tell you how much I value
the exquisite closeness that we have been given.
It is a truly beautiful blessing...

And there will never be a day when I
will take even one moment of that joy and
that sweetness for granted. I know what
a gift you are.

I want you to know it, too.

You have an amazing way of touching
my heart, and you have a way of
turning every day into a time and a
place where the nicest feelings and the
deepest gratitude all come together.

I have such an immense amount of
thanks and appreciation for all this.

And if it's okay with you...
I'd love to go on loving you

forever.